Hello!
I am loving.

I0115145

What makes these animals LOVING?

Everyone loves differently. The animals in this book are loving because they make close long-term relationships with others, show affection, perform mating rituals and show care to those they love.

WARNING!

Remember, even the most loving creatures have their boundaries. Approach with respect. Just because they are loving doesn't mean they won't defend themselves if they feel uneasy. Happy exploring, and may your wild encounters be both loving and safe!

Swans

strong, 'forever' relationships

We are symbols of love across the world.

Swans have heart-shaped neck postures when they try to find a mate.

Swans have elegant dances that they perform together to show their love.

Dolphins

strong social bonds, show affection, and do synchronized swimming together

Dolphins live in social groups called "pods".

Come and jump with me.

They use a variety of vocal noises to communicate with members of their pod.

Otters

life-long pairs, and playful behavior

Otters hold hands while sleeping or floating to stay together.

You're lovely.

Both parents actively raise and protect otter pups.

Elephants

strong family bonds, show affection, and both parents share responsibility

You have a very nice trunk.

Elephants show emotions, like sadness and joy.

Use their voice, body language, and touching to communicate.

Bonobos

strong family bonds, showing affection, and shared parenting responsibilities

Looks clean to me.

Bonobo groups are usually peaceful. They solve problems with empathy instead of fighting.

Bonobos often share food and cooperate to get jobs done.

Cheetahs

small family groups, shared grooming responsibilities

Mother cheetahs are dedicated to taking care of their cubs.

We're the fastest animals in the world, but let's take it easy today.

Brother and sister cheetahs stay together for a long time and support each other.

Owls

life-long pairs and loving parents

Barn owls use a low, soft voice to talk to mates and children.

Your face looks like a heart.

Owl parents take turns taking care of young eggs.

Angelfish

one-on-one relationships and protecting their mates

You're my angel.

Angelfish pairs stay together for a long time.

Mother and father angelfish use their fins to gently fan their eggs, making sure they get enough fresh air.

Red Pandas

close, life-long pairs and fun, social behavior

To attract a mate, red pandas show agility, like tree climbing, branch balancing, leaping and rolling.

You know, red pandas aren't actually pandas.

Seahorses

life-long pairs and shared parenting responsibilities

Thank you for the eggs.

Female seahorses put their eggs in the male's stomach. Then later, the male gives birth to the babies.

Manatees

gentle, loving behavior and close social groups

Did you know, we can live for more than 60 years?

Manatees show love by nuzzling, touching, and even holding tails.

Mandarin Ducks

close, life-long
partnerships

Mandarin ducks are symbols of love in China.

我愛你

They perform a special dance to show how much they care for each other. They twirl around, flap their wings, and even do synchronized movements.

Giraffes

strong social bonds and unique behavior to attract mates

Giraffes have a huge heart. It weighs up to 25 pounds (11kg).

Lovebirds

strong, life-long pair bonds and loving behaviors

Lovebirds are expressive and can make a variety of vocalizations to express their emotions to other birds.

We're so loving, we have "love" in our name.

They often groom and feed each other, and *love* sitting closely together.

Want more?

... and more

COLLECT THEM ALL!
ActiveBrainsBooks.com

Hello parents!

scan here

Visit us to find out about new releases and **FREE** offers. We'll let you know when we have a new release coming out and how you can get it for FREE.

And you can cast your vote for what book we make next!

or visit here

ActiveBrainsBooks.com

scan here

Let us know what you think. As an independent publisher, your honest reviews mean a lot to us and our business. We'd love to hear from you!

or visit here

amazon.com/review/create-review/

FOLLOW US on Amazon.

amazon.com/author/activebrainsbooks

ActiveBrainsBooks.com

ACTIVE BRAINS

www.ingramcontent.com/pod-product-compliance
Lightning Source LLC
Chambersburg PA
CBHW060844270326
41933CB00003B/187